EDGE BOOKS

DOG OWNERSHIP

DOG CARE

Feeding Your Pup a Healthy Diet and Other Dog Care Tips

By Tammy Gagne

Consultant:
Jennifer Zablotny, DVM
Member, American Veterinary
Medical Association

CAPSTONE PRESS
a capstone imprint

Edge Books are published by Capstone Press,
151 Good Counsel Drive, P.O. Box 669, Mankato, Minnesota 56002.
www.capstonepub.com

Library of Congress Cataloging-in-Publication Data
Gagne, Tammy.
  Dog care : feeding your pup a healthy diet and other dog care tips / by Tammy
    Gagne.
    p. cm. — (Edge books: dog ownership)
  Includes bibliographical references and index.
  Summary: "Describes information and tips on dog care"—Provided by publisher.
  ISBN 978-1-4296-6527-8 (library binding)
  1. Dogs—Juvenile literature. 2. Dogs—Health—Juvenile literature. I. Title.
  SF427.G244 2012
  636.7—dc22
                                                        2011003796

Editorial Credits
Angie Kaelberer, editor; Bobbie Nuytten and Ashlee Suker, designers;
    Marcie Spence, media researcher; Eric Manske, production specialist

Photo Credits
Alamy Images: Juniors Bildarchiv, 1, Richard G. Bingham II, 19; Capstone
Studio: Karon Dubke, 6, 9, 16, 21, 22, 23, 26; iStockphoto: dageldog, 13,
MarkHatfield, cover; Shutterstock: Gina Smith, 4, hd connelly, design element,
Lisa Fischer, design element, Margo Harrison, 15, Milada Cistinova, 14,
Phase4Photography, 25, stocksock, design element, Vitelle, 29, Zuzule, 10

Printed in the United States of America in Stevens Point, Wisconsin.
302011   006111WZF11

Table of Contents

CHAPTER 1 Eating Right

Dogs make wonderful additions to their owners' lives. They are always there to play, cuddle, or just spend time with their families. All they ask in return is an owner who cares for them.

As your dog's owner, you are responsible for your pet's food, exercise, and grooming. Your pet also needs to spend time with you. By taking care of these needs, you become the most important person in your dog's life.

Nutrition and Your Dog

Just like people, dogs need healthy food every day. Protein helps dogs grow and fight off disease. Carbohydrates and fat provide energy. Vitamin D and calcium build strong bones and teeth. Vitamin C helps fight off infections. Dogs must also drink plenty of water to carry these nutrients throughout their bodies.

Kibble stays fresh longer than canned dog food does.

nutrient—a substance needed by a living thing to stay healthy

Long ago most dog owners fed their pets table scraps. This diet lacked balance. Dogs ate too much of one nutrient one day but not enough the next. Some foods even made dogs sick.

Today most dogs eat kibble or canned dog food. The best dog foods are made from lean meats and vegetables. Avoid buying foods that contain animal by-products. These parts of an animal, such as chicken beaks and feet, don't provide pets with the nutrition they need.

Special Diets

Some owners make their dogs' meals. Dogs can eat many of the same foods that people do, such as meats, whole grains, and vegetables. But owners must learn which nutrients their dogs need before starting these feeding plans. If you are considering cooking for your dog, talk to your veterinarian first.

Dogs may need different food depending on their age, activity level, or health needs. Puppy food contains more protein than adult food. It also comes in small pieces that puppies can chew easily. Dogs that have allergies need hypoallergenic food. Dogs age 7 or older eat food made for senior pets. Most senior foods are lower in protein than adult foods.

It's safe to occasionally share a healthy snack with your dog. Don't feed your dog chips or other unhealthy foods, though. Some foods are harmful to dogs. Never give your dog chocolate, onions, or anything that contains caffeine.

hypoallergenic—having a quality that reduces or eliminates allergic reactions

Treats are fine, but don't give your dog too many.

DOG DATA

Raw carrots make excellent training treats.

How Often and How Much

Most dogs should eat twice each day—once in the morning and again in the evening. Puppies should eat more often, usually three times a day. Eating often is especially important for puppies of toy breeds like Chihuahuas and Yorkshire terriers. If they don't eat often enough, these puppies can develop **hypoglycemia**.

Puppies need to eat more often than adult dogs do.

hypoglycemia—low blood sugar

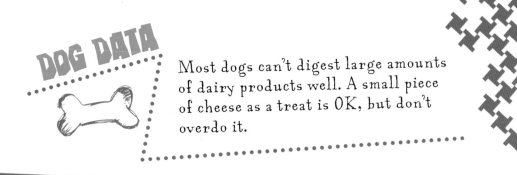
The amount of food a dog should eat depends on its body size, weight, and activity level. Ask your veterinarian how much food your dog should have each day.

Overweight dogs are more likely to suffer from heart disease and diabetes. Too much weight is also hard on a dog's hips and joints. Remember that even healthy treats add extra calories. Low-fat, low-calorie dog food helps overweight dogs return to a healthy weight.

To check your dog's weight, place one hand on each side of your dog's chest and gently push inward. You should easily feel your pet's ribs. If you don't, your dog is probably overweight. But if you can feel the ribs without any effort, your pet may not be eating enough.

Working dogs or those that compete in sports burn more calories than other dogs do. Pet food companies make food just for these athletic animals.

CHAPTER 2 Exercise

Exercise is as important to your dog's health as it is to yours. Dogs that run and play each day stay fit. Regular exercise also helps keep your pet from becoming bored.

Small breeds like Chihuahuas can get all the exercise they need indoors. But even small dogs enjoy getting outside for fresh air and playtime. If your dog is a larger breed, getting outdoors each day is a must. Some large breeds, like the Saint Bernard and Siberian husky, seem to enjoy being outdoors as much as possible.

How you choose to exercise your dog is far less important than doing it. Labrador retrievers enjoy swimming, while greyhounds are fast runners. Almost all dogs seem to enjoy chasing balls or flying discs.

All dogs need exercise, but it's especially important for large breeds.

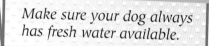

Make sure your dog always has fresh water available.

Always bring a bottle of drinking water and a travel bowl when heading outdoors with your dog. You may notice that your pet drinks more water when it's hot outside. A dog has only a few sweat glands, mostly in its feet. Dogs release excess heat by panting. Panting is a sign that your dog needs to rest and drink water.

DOG DATA

Dogs need to warm up before exercising. Be sure to walk your dog before running or competing in any sports.

Organized Exercise

Organized activities are a great way to exercise your dog. These events can also help your dog with socialization.

If your dog learns new things quickly, it may enjoy rally obedience. In this sport, dogs and handlers move through a course of 10 to 20 stations, performing different exercises at each one.

Breeds such as the Australian shepherd and border collie do well at flyball. In this sport, teams of four dogs perform a relay race as they run through hurdles and catch balls.

Dogs that like to run and jump often enjoy agility. This event includes running across balance beams, jumping through hoops, and even zooming through chutes.

Dogs can earn titles at agility competitions.

CHAPTER 3 Grooming

Clean dogs look and feel much better than dirty ones. Grooming is also important to your pet's health. Brushing and bathing give you a chance to check your dog for signs of illness or injury.

No More Tangles

All dogs need to be brushed regularly. Brushing helps remove dead hair and dirt from your dog's skin. Shorthaired dogs should be brushed about once a week with a soft-bristled brush or grooming mitt. Dogs with long hair must be brushed daily with a slicker brush to prevent tangles. Always brush your dog before a bath.

If your dog has tangles or mats in its fur, be gentle when removing them. Use a detangling spray before slowly combing through the fur. If the fur is very matted, you may need to take your dog to a professional groomer.

Bath Time

How often you should bathe your dog depends on its coat type. Unless a Rottweiler gets extremely dirty, its smooth coat needs a bath only every two or three months. But a long-haired breed like a cocker spaniel should have a bath every four to six weeks. Also, dogs that spend lots of time outdoors will get dirty faster and need more baths.

Always use shampoo made for dogs. Human shampoo can make your dog's skin too dry. Some dog shampoos are made for specific coat colors or types.

The best place to bathe your pet is the bathtub. The water should be lukewarm. Hot water can burn your dog, and cold water can cause chills. Be careful if you bathe your dog outside with a garden hose. The water in a hose that has been sitting in the sun can become very hot. Avoid outdoor bathing when it is chilly or windy. If your dog seems frightened by the hose, stop at once.

Small dogs can even be bathed in large sinks.

After wetting your dog's coat, gently work the shampoo through the fur with your hands or a washcloth. Next, rinse the shampoo from your dog's coat. You can do this with a cup or with a spray nozzle. Rinse twice to make sure all the soap is gone.

Try to make baths a fun experience from the beginning. Bathe your puppy regularly so it can see there is nothing scary about a bath.

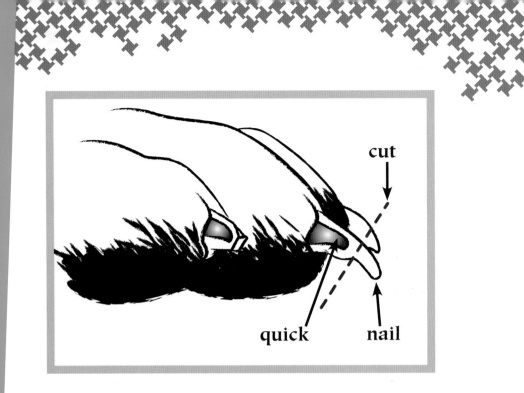

cut

quick nail

Toenail Trimming

If you can hear your dog's nails click when it walks across the floor, they are too long. Trim your dog's toenails every few weeks. Trimming helps prevent your dog from scratching itself, other pets, or people. Also, long nails can make walking painful.

Be careful not to cut your dog's nails to the quick, which causes pain and bleeding. Many owners prefer to have a vet or groomer trim their dogs' nails for this reason.

quick—the tissue under a dog's nail

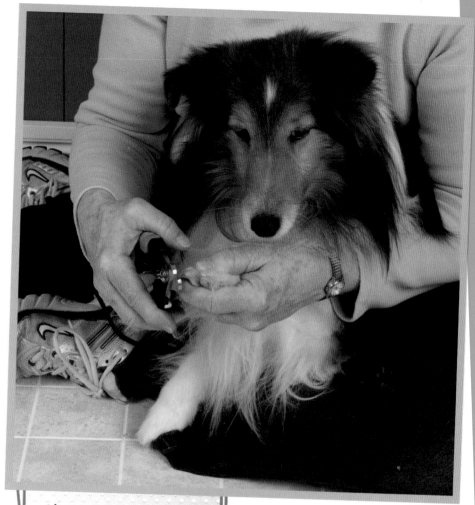

Always use a nail clipper made for dogs.

DOG DATA

If you accidentally cut your dog's quick, applying styptic powder or cornstarch to the wound will help stop the bleeding.

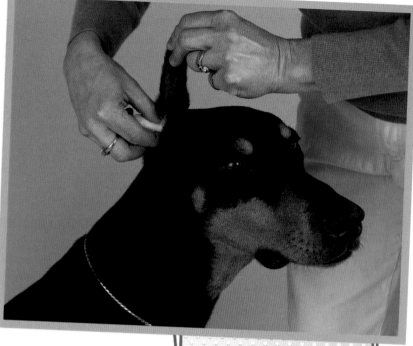

Clean ears are less likely to become infected.

Clean Ears

The best way to prevent ear infections is to keep your dog's ears clean and dry. Use a liquid cleaning solution about once a week. Squirt a small amount of cleaner into your pet's ear. Then wipe the dirt and wax away with a clean cotton ball. Never use a cotton swab in the ear. It can injure your pet.

Doggie Dental

Owners should brush their dogs' teeth every day with toothpaste made for dogs. Toothpaste made for people can make dogs sick. Brushing removes plaque and tartar. These substances can cause infections and even heart problems as bacteria travels through the dog's body.

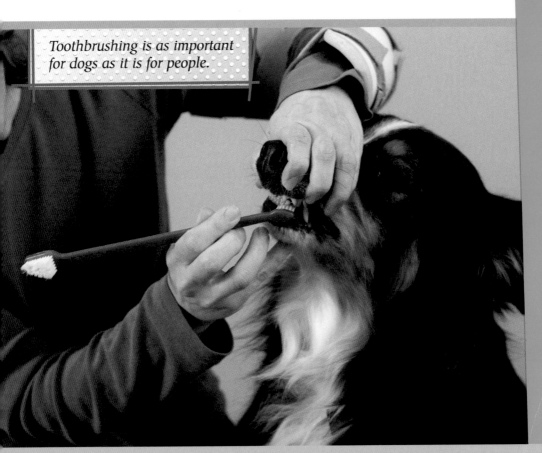

Toothbrushing is as important for dogs as it is for people.

plaque—a colorless film on teeth that causes tooth decay

tartar—the hardened form of plaque

CHAPTER 4

Veterinary Care

Your dog's veterinarian is your best partner in keeping your dog healthy. Regular vet visits help prevent illnesses. They also help identify any problems before they become bigger issues.

Make your dog's first vet appointment as soon as you bring it home. During this exam, the vet will check your dog's weight, temperature, teeth, eyes, ears, and coat. The vet will also give your dog any needed vaccinations. These shots help prevent diseases such as parvovirus and rabies.

Puppies need a number of vaccinations during their first few months of life. Your dog should visit the vet each year for a checkup and any needed booster shots.

Unless you are planning to breed your dog, you should have your pet spayed or neutered. Spayed and neutered dogs won't produce unwanted puppies. They are also less likely to get some forms of cancer.

parvovirus—a dog disease that causes fever, vomiting, diarrhea, and sometimes death

An Ounce of Prevention

You can help keep your dog healthy by using preventive medications. Heartworms, which are transmitted by mosquitoes, can kill a dog. Heartworms and other parasites like fleas and ticks can be prevented by a monthly dose of medicine.

Some flea and tick preventatives are applied between the shoulder blades.

parasite—a small organism that lives on or inside a person or animal

Watch your pet for any changes in behavior. Finding illness early is the best way to keep it from becoming a bigger problem. Scratching is usually the first sign of a food allergy. Stiff, painful movements are a symptom of arthritis. Vomiting or diarrhea is often a sign of parasites or infection.

Not every health danger comes in the form of disease. Many household items are poisonous to pets. Eating only a few holly berries can make your dog sick. Lapping up a few tablespoons of antifreeze can kill it. Your vet can give you a list of plants and other items that are harmful to dogs.

Finally, don't forget that your dog's mental health is just as important as its physical fitness. One of the most important things you can do is spend time with your pet. Dogs are very social animals. By making time for everything your dog needs, you show your pet how important it is to you.

DOG DATA

Other common household items that are harmful to dogs include grapes, raisins, avocados, and the artificial sweetener found in sugarless candy and gum.

Good care helps you and your dog share many happy years together.

GLOSSARY

hypoallergenic (hye-poh-a-luhr-JEN-ik)—having a quality that reduces or eliminates allergic reactions

hypoglycemia (hye-poh-glye-SEE-mee-uh)—low blood sugar

nutrient (NOO-tree-uhnt)—a substance needed by a living thing to stay healthy

parasite (PA-ruh-site)—a small organism that lives on or inside a person or animal; many parasites spread disease

parvovirus (PAHR-voh-vye-ruhss)—a highly contagious disease in dogs that causes fever, vomiting, diarrhea, and sometimes death

plaque (PLAK)—a colorless film on teeth that contains bacteria and causes tooth decay

quick (KWIK)—the sensitive tissue underneath a fingernail or toenail

tartar (TAHR-tuhr)—the hardened form of plaque and minerals on teeth

READ MORE

Adelman, Beth. *Good Dog!: Dog Care for Kids.* Chanhassen, Minn.: Child's World, 2007.

Buchwald, Claire. *Are You Ready for Me?* Sit! Stay! Read! Edina, Minn.: Gryphon Press, 2009.

Niven, Felicia Lowenstein. *Learning to Care for a Dog.* Beginning Pet Care with American Humane Society. Berkeley Heights, N.J.: Enslow, 2010.

Zobel, Derek. *Caring for Your Dog.* Blastoff! Readers Pet Care Library. Minneapolis: Bellwether Media, 2010.

INTERNET SITES

FactHound offers a safe, fun way to find Internet sites related to this book. All of the sites on FactHound have been researched by our staff.

Here's all you do:

Visit *www.facthound.com*

Type in this code: 9781429665278

Check out projects, games and lots more at **www.capstonekids.com**

INDEX

DATE DUE

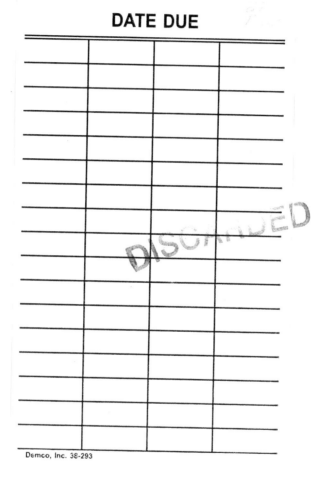

Demco, Inc. 38-293